# THE CHANGING FACE OF
# MALAYSIA

## Text by AIDEN GLENDINNING and JIM HOLMES
## Photographs by JIM HOLMES

HODDER
Wayland

an imprint of Hodder Children's Books

© 2004 White-Thomson Publishing Ltd

Produced for Hodder Wayland by
White-Thomson Publishing Ltd
2/3 St Andrew's Place
Lewes BN7 1UP

Editor: Elaine Fuoco-Lang
Copy editor: Alison Cooper
Designer: Clare Nicholas
Concept Design: Chris Halls, Mind's Eye Design
Consultant: Ian Elgie

First published in Great Britain in 2004 by Hodder Wayland, an imprint of
Hodder Children's Books.

British Library Cataloguing in Publication Data
Glendinning, Aiden
    The Changing Face of Malaysia
    1. Human geography – Malaysia – Juvenile literature
    2. Malaysia – History – Juvenile literature  3. Malaysia – Social life and
    customs – Juvenile literature
    I. Title  II. Holmes, Jim  III. Malaysia
    959.5'054

ISBN 0 7502 4269 8

Printed in China

Hodder Children's Books
A division of Hodder Headline Limited
338 Euston Road, London NW1 3BH

**Acknowledgements**
The publishers would like to thank
the following for their contributions
to this book: Rob Bowden – statistics
research; Peter Bull – map
illustration; Nick Hawken – statistics
panel illustrations. All photographs
are by Jim Holmes.

# Contents

# Pinang – Pearl of the Orient

Since the sixteenth century, the island of Pinang has been a gateway to business in Southeast Asia. By 1786 the East India Company, whose business expansion laid the foundations of the British Empire, had made it a major trading post. George Town, the main port, soon became a bustling centre for commerce, attracting traders from all over the east. Visitors fell in love with Pinang's beauty and the island became known as the 'Pearl of the Orient'.

▲ *Locals in George Town, Pinang often meet up for a chat at tea stalls.*

Pinang's importance in world trade declined as nearby Singapore grew bigger. After Malaysia gained independence from Britain in 1957, business boomed again. Tourism became a major source of income for the island. The government also saw it as the perfect place to develop new high-tech industries, and the number of computer-chip factories and semiconductor plants now on Pinang has led some people to call it 'Silicon Island'.

The recent rapid development of industry and tourism has caused a lot of concern in Pinang. Fishermen complain that marine life is badly affected, and the number of tourists is falling as the island's beauty is spoiled. Today, the 'Pearl of the Orient' faces some stiff challenges.

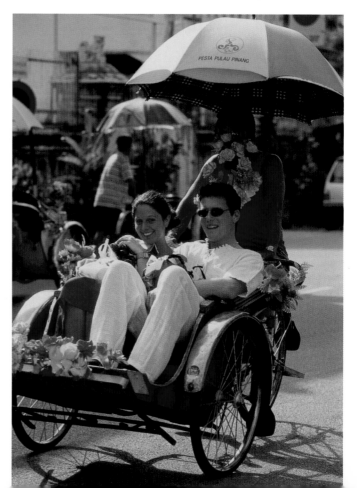

▶ *Tourists enjoy a relaxing ride in an old trishaw through the narrow streets of George Town, Pinang.*

▲ This map shows the main geographical features of Malaysia, as well as most of the places mentioned in this book.

# MALAYSIA: KEY FACTS

**Area:** 329,847 sq km

**Population:** 24.01 million (mid-2002 estimate)

**Population density:** 73 people per sq km

**Capital city:** Kuala Lumpur (1.3 million)

**Other main cities:** Ipoh (0.53 million), Petaling Jaya (0.43 million), Johor Baharu (0.40 million), Kota Kinabula (0.35 million)

**Highest mountain:** Mount Kinabalu (4,101 m)

**Longest river:** Rajang (567 km); Kinabatangan (560 km)

**Main language:** Bahasa Malayu

**Major religions:** Islam (52 per cent), Buddhism (17 per cent), Taoism (12 per cent), Christianity (8 per cent), Hinduism (8 per cent), Animism (3 per cent)

**Money:** Malaysian ringgit (1 ringgit = 100 sen)

# 2 Past Times

About 4,500 years ago groups of people whom historians call the Proto Malays moved to the south-east of Asia from China, joining the aboriginal peoples already there. Migration waves from India, China, Siam and Arab lands in the Middle East, mixed with the Proto Malays to create a loose grouping known as the Deutero Malays. The Deutero Malays mixed with Indonesian groups to form the Malays.

Early Indian and Greek writers called the Malay peninsula the 'Land of Gold' because of its rich trade. Malay rulers adopted many customs from Indian and Chinese traders, including the Hindu religion, and, later on, Buddhism. Islam was introduced in the fifteenth century as a result of contact with Arab merchants.

▲ Most Malay females wear Islamic dress when out in public.

European powers established colonies in Malay ports to control the rich trade in gold, wood, spices and tin. From the nineteenth century Malaya was under British control, although it was captured by the Japanese during the Second World War from 1939–1945.

◄ Modern Kuala Lumpur is a city with an exciting mix of architecture. This is the Jamek mosque in downtown Kuala Lumpur.

## Malaya to Malaysia

Malaya won independence from Britain in 1957 and Tunku Abdul Rahman became the country's first Prime Minister. In 1961 Singapore, Sabah and Sarawak joined Malaya in a federal union called Malaysia, although Singapore left the union in 1965. The country struggled through a three-year confrontation with Indonesia, and later with clashes between its Malay and Chinese communities, before establishing a stable state. Since the 1980s Malaysia has experienced tremendous growth and prosperity, with new industries creating a wealthier and more peaceful society.

▶ *The Petronas twin towers, headquarters of the state oil company, are one of the tallest buildings in the world and a symbol of Malaysia's economic progress.*

# IN THEIR OWN WORDS

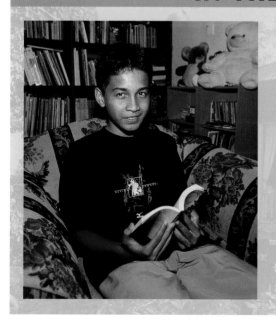

'My name is Mohammed Amer bin Imran, and I live in Kota Baharu. I am 16 years old. My grandad always tells me how hard life was when he was growing up and what it was like being a prisoner of the Japanese during the Second World War. I want to be a doctor when I get older, just like my mother and father. I want to help people if I can. My grandparents did not get much chance at higher education, so I feel lucky that I can study as much as I want. Kota Baharu town is much bigger now than it used to be. It's more modern and convenient with more hospitals, roads and public transport. Who knows what Malaysia might achieve in the future – maybe we will even send somebody into space!'

# 3

# Landscape and Climate

Malaysia is separated into two regions, divided by the South China Sea: Peninsular Malaysia, also called West Malaysia, and East Malaysia. Thirteen *negeri*, or states, and three federal territories comprise the Federation of Malaysia. Together with its islands, the country is almost the same size as Norway, or the US state of New Mexico.

Peninsular Malaysia is part of mainland South-east Asia. It is the more developed part of the country, where most of the major cities are located. It is bordered by Thailand to the north, with the Andaman Sea along its west coast and the South China Sea to the east. Singapore lies at its southern tip, connected by a bridge known as the causeway.

▼ *Mist covers the forests of Malaysia.*

East Malaysia's states of Sabah and Sarawak cover the northern half of Borneo. Borneo is a huge island on which Brunei and the Indonesian province of Kalimantan are also located. The people of East Malaysia are mostly from ethnic groups quite different from the Malays of the West.

## Mountains and coastal plains

The southern part of Peninsular Malaysia is relatively flat, but the north contains several mountain ranges, including the Cameron Highlands, whose cool forests are popular with visitors. At 4,101 m, Mount Kinabalu in Sabah is the highest peak in South-east Asia.

Along the coasts of the peninsula are ancient mangrove forests full of rare plants. There is a wide, fertile plain on the west coast, and a narrow coastal plain on the east. However, the amount of forest and mountain means that there is not much land available for farming. As the population grows, development threatens natural features such as the rainforests and rivers.

▼ *This mangrove forest is a national park. The walkways allow visitors to explore the rich but wet environment.*

# IN THEIR OWN WORDS

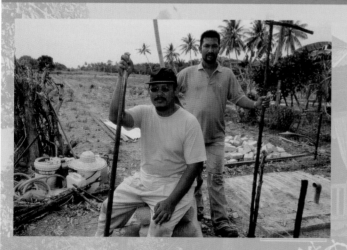

'I am Roslan (on the left) and I am a farmer from Pinang Island. I suppose any work is hard really, but farming seems to be one of the hardest jobs. Times have really changed in Malaysia and there has been a big shift from agriculture to technology and other industries. We are building an underground water tank here. There used to be a stream that ran past the edge of the field, and we could grow crops all year round. Then, a few months ago, the stream just dried up. Without a steady flow of water, how can the farm survive? If you set your mind to it though, you can do anything. As the environment changes we have to change too and develop.'

## Ancient forests

The tropical rainforests that cover 61 per cent of Malaysia are thought to be the oldest in the world. They were too far away from the ice sheets of the last Ice Age to be affected by the low temperatures, meaning that they are around 130 million years old. These forests cover an area almost as big as the whole United Kingdom.

## Plentiful water

The country's two longest rivers, the Rajang (567 km) and the Kinabatangan (560 km), are in East Malaysia. Many of the steep mountain slopes of Sarawak and Sabah receive over 5,000 mm of rain per year, and fast-flowing rivers rush down the mountains. These can be dammed to provide hydroelectric power: most of Malaysia's lakes were created by dam projects.

▲ *The forests in the Titiwangsa mountain range near Fraser's Hill are amongst Malaysia's greatest treasures.*

## Sticky weather

The tropical climate is hot and humid all year round. Two monsoons sweep into the country from its long coastlines (4,675 km in total) almost all year round, drenching the plains and Malaysia's many mountains. There is no cold season and average daily temperatures are between 20° and 30° C. There is so much water in the air that humidity is usually around 90 per cent, making daily life rather sticky. It is this constant climate that produced and maintains Malaysia's famous rainforests, which teem with animal and plant life.

▶ *Malaysia's tropical rainstorms can be very heavy.*

# IN THEIR OWN WORDS

'My name is Dr Adzmi Yacoub and I'm a soil scientist from Taman Negra, near Kuala Lumpur. Soil is so important to us – basically it's what plants survive on. Soil is a very thin layer on top of the earth's rocks and the deeper the soil, the better it should be. Soil is very fragile: when you take out trees – for logging, for example – you have to be careful not to disturb the topsoil. Roots hold the soil in place even on steep slopes, and if you are not careful you can get terrible landslides that cause a lot of damage after the trees have been chopped down. Heavy rainfall makes the problem even worse and we can get up to 4,000 mm of rain in a four-month period.'

# 4

# Natural Resources

### Powering the nation

Although oil was first discovered in the country in 1882, it was not until the 1970s that Malaysia began drilling in the sea and started to produce large quantities of petroleum and natural gas. After the world oil crisis of 1973, the government took control of these valuable resources and created the Petronas state company to manage them. Crude oil is refined into petrol and other products, mainly at big terminals in Sarawak. The country currently exports petroleum, but the oil reserves are not huge and Malaysian people use more petrol every year. By 2008, the country could be using more oil than it can produce. The oil wells could be dry by 2020 and scientists are trying to find ways to switch to solar power and biomass fuel made from palm oil. While over 90 per cent of electricity is still generated from non-renewable fossil fuels such as oil and coal, use of hydroelectricity is increasing and there are plans to create many more dams.

▼ *Car drivers fill up with LNG, liquid natural gas, which is much cheaper than petrol and is a by-product of oil exploration.*

## Wealth from the earth

Tin has been exported from the Malay peninsula for centuries. Kuala Lumpur, the capital, was founded by 87 Chinese tin miners in 1857, in the middle of huge deposits of the metal. Products made from pewter (a mixture of tin and lead), especially from Selangor province, are still a valuable export but tin mining has declined in Malaysia. Rubber trees, which produce the resin that is made into rubber, used to be a very valuable natural resource but that industry is also now in decline. Timber remains an important industry, with a lot of wood still cut from the forests of East Malaysia for sale.

▲ *Although natural rubber from trees has been replaced by synthetic products in many industries, big rubber plantations still exist.*

## IN THEIR OWN WORDS

'I'm Mohammed, a taxi driver from Kuala Lumpur, and I am 29 years old. I drive a car powered by natural gas that I can get from a Petronas service station. Petronas is a very big company and their service stations are everywhere. It's also a Malaysian company, so it helps the country if we buy from them. Most taxis run on natural gas because it is half the price of petrol. People tell me it is also cleaner and doesn't make so much pollution, which must be a good thing.'

## Plantations

Palm oil is made from the fruit and kernels of the oil palm tree. With over two million hectares devoted to growing palm trees, Malaysia is the largest producer of palm oil in the world. Ninety per cent of it is used to make cooking oil and food products, but the government is promoting ways of converting the oil to other uses, such as soap, cosmetics and plastics. Most importantly, palm oil will be used to replace diesel, both in motor engines and in industry.

Another 1.5 million hectares are covered with huge rubber plantations, which used to be the biggest agricultural industry. As land has been converted to growing oil palm and other crops, Thailand has replaced Malaysia as the number one producer of natural rubber. In addition, many industries have switched to using synthetic rubber.

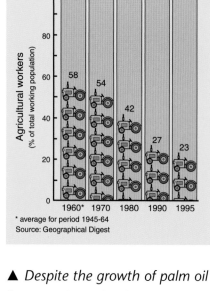

Agricultural workers (% of total working population)

| 1960* | 1970 | 1980 | 1990 | 1995 |
|-------|------|------|------|------|
| 58 | 54 | 42 | 27 | 23 |

* average for period 1945-64
Source: Geographical Digest

▲ Despite the growth of palm oil farms Malaysia's reliance on agriculture halved between 1970 and 1990, and is still falling.

◀ Oil palms on the edge of a plantation near Taiping.

▼ Palm fruit: this is squeezed to produce the oil used in many food products, including margarine.

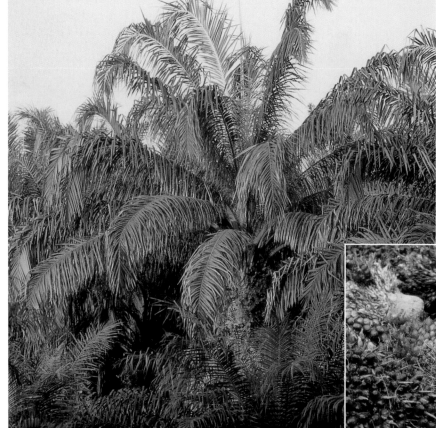

## Farming and fishing

Since the rubber industry began to decline, many farmers with small areas of land have started to grow more cash crops such as cacao, sugar-cane, coconuts and pineapples. Rice forms the staple diet, but people grow it mainly to feed themselves and their families rather than for sale. Fish and seafood are very popular, and many people earn a living on fishing boats along Malaysia's long coasts. However, catches are declining and some fishermen blame this on pollution. To try to protect fish stocks, the government has stopped issuing new licences for fishing boats. Although Malaysia is mainly a Muslim nation and Muslims do not eat pork, it is the biggest producer of pork in the region. Ethnic Chinese farmers run this industry, which survived a terrible outbreak of disease among its pigs in the late 1990s.

▶ *A small pepper tree orchard climbs this hillside. Pepper used to be a huge crop in Malaysia but production is now falling.*

# IN THEIR OWN WORDS

'I'm Abdul Wahab Ismail and I've been growing rubber for almost 25 years. I work at my plantation, just outside Taiping. A few years ago the rubber price was terrible, always going down, but it's a little better these days. Before, we would collect rubber resin from the trees, make it into rubber mats ourselves, then sell it. Now we just sell the resin to middlemen, often processing companies from Singapore. Rubber plantations are being taken over by oil palm. Maybe there's not so much need for real rubber any more, but the future is bright for palm oil industries. I don't know who will run the farms in future though. Young people don't want to work on farms these days – they want to work in factories or offices, where they earn more money and don't get burnt by the sun.'

# 5

# The Changing Environment

### The cost to nature

Although Malaysia still has large forests, there is growing concern at the number of trees being cut down in the country. Some people say the timber is being cut down four times as quickly as it would take to grow back again. Many of the accusations of overlogging come from outside the country. The government has responded to such claims by saying that countries that have already destroyed their own ancient forests have no right to criticize Malaysia.

Hydroelectric dams, which Malaysia is building to reduce fossil fuel use, are also controversial. In 2001 the government decided to go ahead with construction of the huge Bakun hydroelectric power project in Sarawak. This could destroy 27,600 hectares of rainforest. Another threat to the forests comes from fires started by farmers who use the traditional slash-and-burn method of rice growing. Loss of forests threatens wildlife and leads to flood problems.

▲ *Huge logs are being transported out of the forest. Both natural forests and old rubber tree plantations are making way for construction and development.*

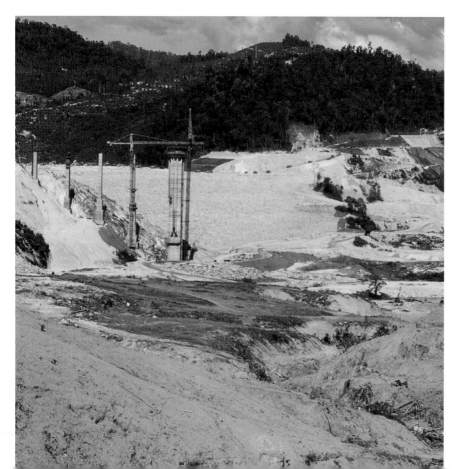

◀ *A new dam under construction. There are environmental benefits as well as problems related to the building of dams.*

# IN THEIR OWN WORDS

'My name is Apin. I am 22 years old. I live in the village of Kampong Pertak. The village has been rebuilt in a new location because a dam is being built and the lake would have flooded our old homes. They have cut down the forest to sell the wood before they make the lake. Our old houses were made of wood and bamboo. We made them ourselves, but these houses are made of concrete. Most of us liked the old ones best. We have water in the taps now, but we still like to wash in the river. I sometimes wonder what will happen to me and my village in the future.'

## Muddied waters

The growth of cities and industries has made it difficult for Malaysia to manage the increase in sewage and waste from factories and farms. Water pollution is affecting many of the country's coastal waters and rivers. Fishermen have complained about property developments that reclaim land along the coast so that it can be built on. This can drastically affect tidal patterns, creating problems for fishermen. In addition, companies that dump industrial waste and mud into the sea are killing fish stocks. The government has introduced various laws to try to tackle the problem, but seems to have difficulty in protecting fragile ecosystems against business and development.

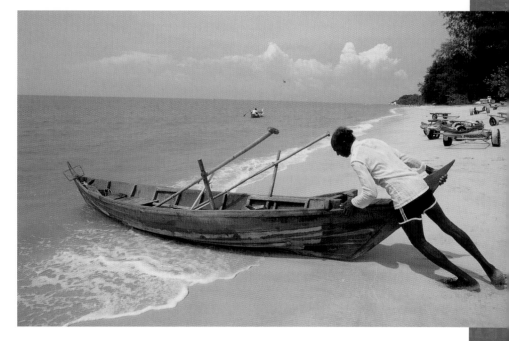

▲ *Although this water on the coast of Pinang looks clear, the increase in tourism to the island is causing the water to become more polluted.*

### The growing cities

No city in Malaysia has grown as much as the capital, Kuala Lumpur, which now has a population of over 1.3 million. The city, often known simply as KL, has now stretched out to meet its neighbouring towns, forming an urban conurbation called Kelang Valley. Many workers commute from the surrounding state of Selangor, whose population grew by over 60 per cent between 1980 and 1991. Other big growth areas include Sabah and Johor Baharu.

◄ *As the city grows, high-tech light rail systems are being introduced to try to reduce pollution and traffic jams.*

Fifty-four per cent of Malaysians are now thought to live in urban areas, with more moving in from the countryside every year. The growth in population means that services such as transport, housing and water systems in Kuala Lumpur and the other popular cities are struggling to cope. The government is trying to reduce the growth of big cities by encouraging people to move to different areas. One of these areas is Putrajaya, 25 km south of Kuala Lumpur, which is going to become the new capital. Government offices are being moved there from crowded Kuala Lumpur.

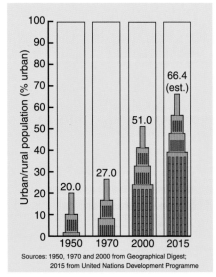

Sources: 1950, 1970 and 2000 from Geographical Digest; 2015 from United Nations Development Programme

▲ *More and more people are moving to the cities in Malaysia, and the figures are still growing.*

## Hazy city

As it grows, Kuala Lumpur has become infamous for its traffic jams and air pollution. In recent years the situation has become almost unbearable as haze from forest fires in Borneo and Indonesia has drifted over the city, blocking out sunlight. Much of the capital's pollution comes from thousands of motorbikes, which are popular in South-east Asia. The cheaper motorbikes have engines that create a lot of noise and smoke. Steps have been taken to improve public transport and so reduce pollution: there are three new metro systems, which are being expanded.

▼ *Traffic pollution and the burning of forests in rural areas cause the haze in the air over Kuala Lumpur.*

# IN THEIR OWN WORDS

'My name is Stella Tan Pei Zin. That's me in the middle with my friends Tan Tiong Shek and Samantha Tan. At school, in Kuching, we study recycling in science lessons, but we have only done a few projects. On television they encourage us to collect things and hand them into recycling centres that have been set up. Some of the materials can be used again, and others may be dangerous for the environment. Plastics take a long time to break down and you can see bags and other things scattered in the countryside.'

## Protecting paradise

Although Malaysia is the world's biggest exporter of tropical hardwoods, some measures have been taken to protect its forests for future generations. The law declares that 69 per cent of the remaining forest area is Permanent Forest Estate, with strict rules on how many trees can be cut per hectare, and the size of trees that may be felled. In addition, 12 per cent of the forests are now Totally Protected Areas, forming the country's national parks and reserves.

Tourism has become big business in Malaysia, and many visitors come to see the amazing rain forests. The astonishing variety of plants and animals they contain also promises to help humankind's health. Scientists have begun searching the wealth of life in Malaysia's forests for new medicines to combat AIDS, cancer and other illnesses.

▼ *Trekkers in the Borneo jungle wait to catch a glimpse of the elusive orangutan. The word orangutan in Malay means 'man of the jungle'.*

### Balancing act

Protecting natural riches like forests and water life is a huge challenge in a country trying to develop economically. The government wants to make money from wood but it also wants to reduce deforestation. One way to do this is to encourage businesses to process logs into sawn timber or furniture. These timber products can be exported for higher prices than cut tree trunks, so fewer trees have to be cut down in order to make money. New plantations, such as teak plantations in the north, are being planted especially for use in the timber industry. The plantation trees can be used in the future so that natural forests are not cut for business.

▲ *Destruction of the forests is being carefully monitored by the government.*

## IN THEIR OWN WORDS

'I'm an ecologist living in Kuching and my name is Anthony Sebastian. Environmental issues are being discussed much more now – people seem to be taking an interest at last. They are even included in the school curriculum. Of course this does not always mean that the real issues are being talked about. An achievement in any country is not just big cars, big houses and money, it is also about having a sense of belonging or ownership. When people begin to understand that all that surrounds them has to be shared and looked after for everybody's benefit, then the environment will have a chance.'

# 6 The Changing Population

## Population explosion

The number of people in Malaysia has virtually doubled since the early 1980s. Although the population continues to grow, the rate of increase has slowed. Improving economic conditions mean people have more income and so do not need so many children to help them grow food or earn money. The government's population programme educates people on the benefits of planning their families and having fewer children. In 1970 Malaysian families each had an average of 5.2 children. By 2000, that figure had dropped to an average of 3.2 children per family.

One reason for the continued population growth is the country's economic success, which has attracted many immigrant workers, particularly from Indonesia, Bangladesh and Pakistan. They come to take low-paid or hard jobs that Malaysians do not want.

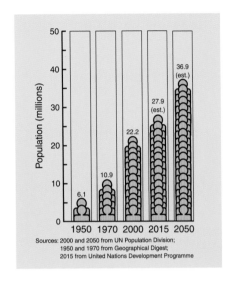

Sources: 2000 and 2050 from UN Population Division;
1950 and 1970 from Geographical Digest;
2015 from United Nations Development Programme

▲ Malaysia's population has more than doubled in recent years and it is predicted to keep increasing, especially in cities such as Kuala Lumpur.

◄ Many families live in high-rise apartment blocks around Kuala Lumpur.

## Longer lives

Life expectancy is also increasing. Malaysia is now a youthful society, but by 2025 it will be an elderly one. In traditional Asian society, families greatly respect the aged and look after them at home. With health facilities improving though, people are living longer and the country will have to look after many more old people in the future. In 1975, Malaysians lived to an average of 63 years old, but now the national life expectancy is over 72 years. In the cities traditional family life is changing fast and even in remote villages the pattern of life is changing. As modern families have fewer children, there will not be so many young working people to care for the elderly people of tomorrow in the way that old people are looked after today.

▼ *The family is very important to Malaysian culture. Here the whole family is on an outing to a Kuala Lumpur park.*

# IN THEIR OWN WORDS

'My name is Payang, of the Bidayuh people. I've lived in Kampung Anna Rais, in Sarawak, for 51 years. Originally we lived in the longhouse with many other families, but I have five children so we built a separate house nearby; many families have done this now. This is a big change in our community – people never used to have separate houses, even though they had more kids before. We are comfortable with our lives. We have always had land and a strong community spirit; we still have a sense of sharing. The youngsters now go out of the community and earn some money, but they almost always come home again. Minority groups used to be a little like second-class citizens and we did not venture out of the community, but now we have adapted to the changes in modern society.'

### Princes and their predecessors

Ethnic Malays, who make up around 50 per cent of society, are known as *bumiputera*, or 'princes of the soil'. Since colonial times, much of Malaysia's business has been controlled by ethnic Chinese. After independence this caused resentment amongst Malays, resulting in race riots. Since then laws have been brought in to give Malays more power in economic life. Every business, education and civil service organization must give a certain percentage of jobs to Malays.

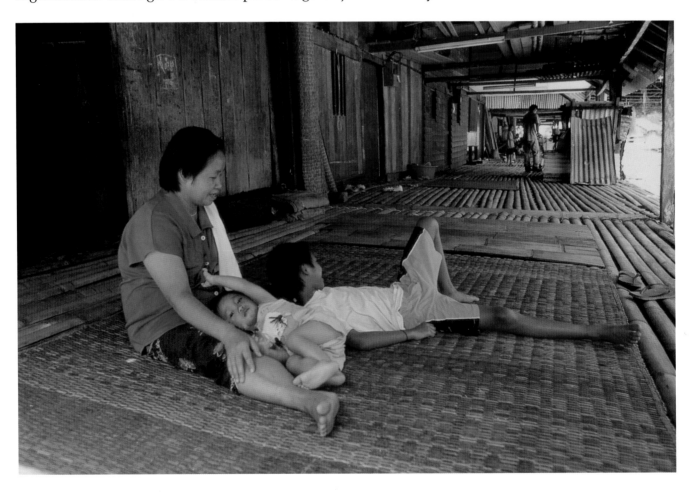

The many ethnic groups who lived in Malaysia long before anyone else are called *orang asal*, the 'original people'. They now form less than 10 per cent of the population. The *orang asal* generally share a strong spiritual tie to the forests, but their lifestyle is changing drastically in some areas as the forests are exploited and social services are provided.

▲ *The Bidayuh people of Borneo traditionally live in 'longhouses', which can be over 100 metres long and house up to 50 families.*

### Economic backbone

The Chinese and Indian communities are often regarded as the country's economic core. As in most of South-east Asia, the Chinese still have great economic power in Malaysia. Many Indians came in colonial times to work on rubber plantations. Although some have been successful in business, many are still poor. Indian and Chinese temples, architecture and food contribute greatly to Malaysian culture. In politics, the Malays have dominated all groups since independence, but there are now many political parties in the country, seeking to represent its entire people.

▲ *A young girl at the Hindu Sri Maha Mariamman temple in Kuala Lumpur.*

## IN THEIR OWN WORDS

'My name is Wong Karhoo and I live in Kuala Lumpur. I am sitting here outside this Chinese temple waiting for my younger sister to finish her English lesson. Many people study extra lessons at temple schools, especially English and mathematics. When I was younger only Chinese kids went to these schools, but now a whole range of kids from all ethnic groups study there. When I returned to Malaysia after studying in the UK, I was really surprised at the huge changes. Even new cities had been started. There are so many opportunities, and as an engineer specializing in plastics it is really exciting to be working on high-quality projects.'

# 7

# Changes at Home

## Family life

The people of Malaysia have a variety of lifestyles. Traditional Malay culture centres on the *kampung*, or village, where respect and obedience towards parents and elders are very important. Order and tradition in the village are strengthened through the influence of the community, led by the village headman. As in many other cultures all over the world though, the traditional ways of life are changing as more and more people move to urban areas. Today, many Malays in the cities are adopting different lifestyles: later marriage and smaller families mean that young people are enjoying greater social freedom and doing fewer home chores.

▼ *Some traditional Malay houses can still be found in the cities.*

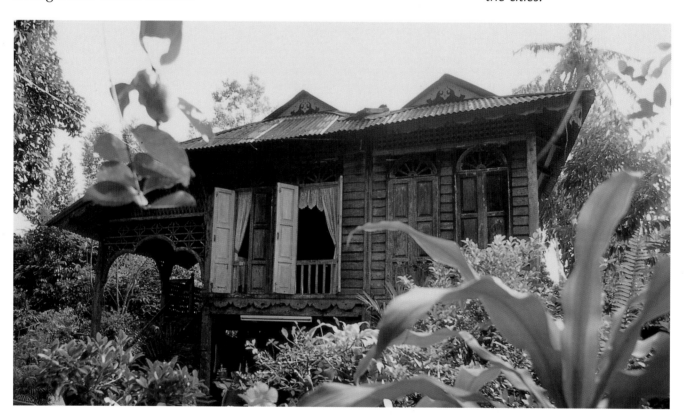

Intermarriage between ethnic groups is increasing, and all groups seem to be moving away from the traditionally strict rules of domestic life. The younger generations are less likely to live in the big family groups that their grandparents knew, and in cities it is very difficult for extended families to stay together.

## Western influence

Western television shows, movies, music and advertising have become popular. Many of the people who see them want to adopt the lifestyles presented by the Western media, which seem more modern and exciting. However, there are also many Malaysians who want to preserve their culture. The government sometimes tries to limit foreign media, while encouraging traditional arts and ways of life.

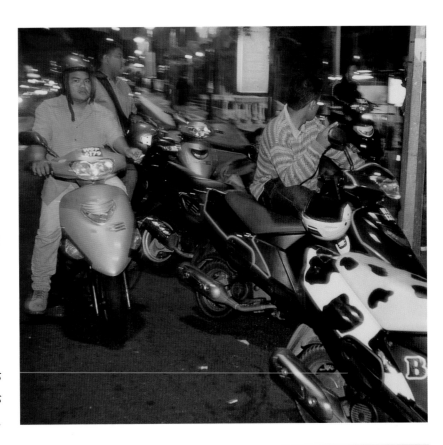

▶ *Young people on motor scooters get together during the early hours of a Kuala Lumpur morning.*

# IN THEIR OWN WORDS

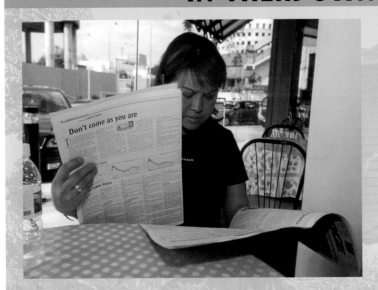

'My name is Faridah Stephens and I live in Kuala Lumpur. In the early 1990s the media situation really changed in Malaysia and many new publications were started. We even got cable TV, which meant we could see overseas programmes. It was very exciting, and gave people a wider view of what was happening in the world. The government gives out licences for media publications, and of course, as in most countries in the world, different publications present the views of different political groups. Newspapers here are printed in the three main languages of the population: Malay, Chinese and Tamil. The Internet has really transformed publishing and public access to information and news. Now people can read so many points of view and learn so many opinions.'

## Women's roles

Changes in the economy and society mean that Malaysian women are generally becoming more independent. Among educated people, there is less pressure to get married and have children at a young age, meaning that women have more opportunities to study and work. Previously, women were lucky if they had the chance to finish primary school. Now more girls than boys finish secondary school and nearly as many girls as boys go on to university.

▼ *A mix of religions and attitudes can be found amongst young people.*

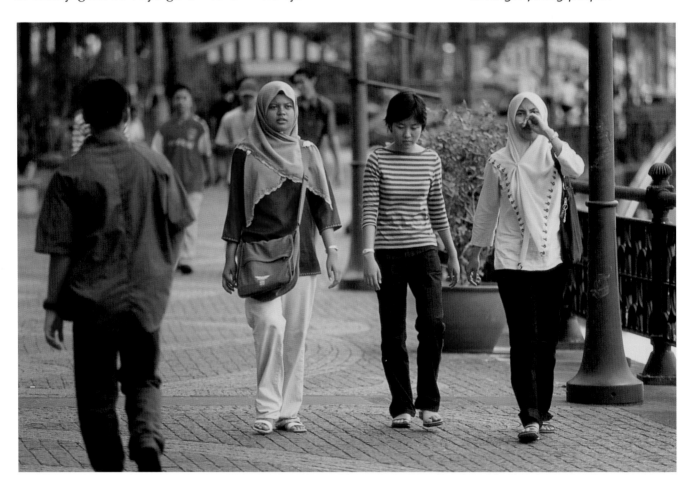

Healthcare for women has also improved. The number of mothers who die during childbirth fell by around 70 per cent between 1980 and 1998. Malaysia as a whole still believes in the importance of the family, and in rural areas, where traditions are strong, people marry early. If an unmarried girl gets pregnant, her family will push her to marry.

# IN THEIR OWN WORDS

'My name is Dr Ainon Mohd Mokhtar and I live in Kuching. I'm the only female physician in this hospital but a lot of women are now doing well in the medical profession. I'm not married. This may be partly due to my career and partly because I want to be independent. People accept the new way is better than before and I don't think I've been pressurized by society. Of course a lot of women still put family before their jobs and choose to become housewives but there are plenty of married women doctors who are able to succeed in both their career and their family lives. Compared to my parents, I should consider myself lucky. During their time, it was common for women to have no basic education.'

## Coming to power

In many Muslim countries women are not allowed to work outside the home, but in Malaysia women have good access to jobs compared with some of their South-east Asian neighbours. Women now make up nearly half the work force. Traditional ideas still protect women in some ways – for example, there is a separate labour law applying to women, stating that they cannot do night shifts or heavy physical work. Over 30 per cent of business and administration managers are women and one of the country's most famous political leaders, Wan Azizah Wan Ismail, is a woman. When she appears in public, Wan Azizah still wears the traditional dress of Malay women, proving that tradition and change can sometimes go hand-in-hand.

▼ *While the roles of Malaysian women may be changing, many still go to the mosque for daily prayers.*

## Education

It is not just women who are benefiting from improved education in Malaysia. The country has made great strides since independence. The state now provides free education for all children aged 6–18 and nearly all children attend primary school. Parents can choose to send their children to primary schools that teach in Bahasa Malayu, Chinese or Tamil, which is the language of most of the ethnic Indian population. Secondary school students must study in Bahasa Malayu, although in some schools certain subjects are also taught in Chinese or Tamil. After independence English was banned from schools, but that has now changed, and all pupils must take English as a second language.

▲ *Learning English at a language college is seen as essential to getting ahead in business in modern Malaysia.*

Further education is increasing, with many students choosing to study sciences and technology. Malaysia now has more than 17 public and private universities, including the National University in Bangi and the University of Technology in Johor Baharu. Some rich families still send their children to foreign universities, but the standard in Malaysia continues to improve.

▶ *A new university campus near Kuching, in Sarawak.*

# IN THEIR OWN WORDS

'My name is Hafsah Mohdzain. I live and work on Pinang Island. I think I always wanted to be a teacher, but I have to be a student for three years before then. I'm in my final year now and have to do my in-school practice as soon as I graduate. I'm a little worried about it actually. I feel children have changed a lot from when I was at school – they seem much more aggressive now. Good teachers are so important though. How are kids going to learn if the teachers are not good? We are a racially mixed country and there are differing attitudes and ideas, but education and teachers are vital to moving the country forward and helping everybody develop.'

In rural areas, obtaining a good education is more difficult. Language can be a problem for some ethnic minorities, who do not have enough teachers or books in their own language and do not speak Bahasa Malayu well. Finding teachers to work in such places can also be a problem. Some international and government organizations promote what is called non-formal education in these areas. This aims to teach ways of improving living standards to people of all ages in whole communities.

▶ *These young girls attend a rural school run by local religious leaders.*

## Diet, health and medicine

Health is another area in which Malaysia has made great advances since the 1970s. In the 1990s government policy included a National Health Programme, which helped to reduce the number of infants who die soon after birth. The programme also educates communities and young people about the benefits of contraception and the dangers of unprotected sex.

Modern hospitals have been set up in towns and cities, and there are more doctors than before, although traditional healers (shamans) and traditional medicine still play an important role. Amongst Malays the shaman is known as a *bomoh*, while the Chinese visit a *sinseh*. Shamans may call on spirits when treating people, or prescribe medicines made from local plants and animal products. Some Chinese medicines are now banned because they come from endangered animals, but Western doctors have started to learn from traditional herblore.

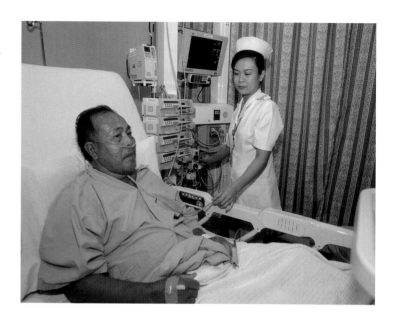

▲ *A modern hospital with state-of-the-art facilities.*

# IN THEIR OWN WORDS

'My name is Nai Anak Lahai, of the Temuan people of East Malaysia. I'm so old the number is lost now. I'm the oldest survivor of my family. We have always been shamans, working with sick people to make them better. I play a special instrument called a *buloh limbong*, made from bamboo, which draws out the evil spirits from a person. Then they get better. Sometimes it takes days and days for this ritual to heal a sick person. I have been playing since I was a small child. It's the only thing I have ever done. These days we don't do it very often. Youngsters still believe we can make them better, but maybe they don't get sick so much these days.'

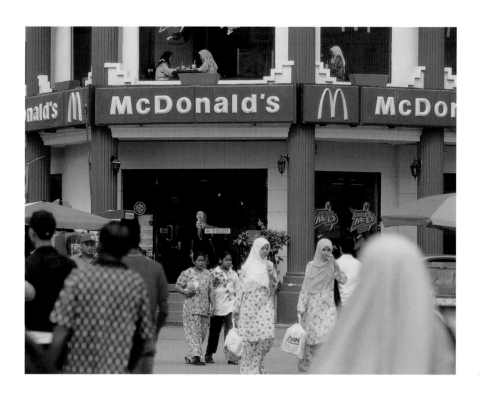

◀ *Fast-food restaurants have become popular in the cities.*

The ethnic mix means that there are several different traditional diets in Malaysia, all of them healthy. The staple foods are rice or cassava, and most protein comes from fish. In cities, Western-style food outlets are becoming popular, though many people prefer local, healthier fast food. Typically, Malaysians eat a lot of fruit and vegetables and alcohol consumption is low. Muslim Malays are forbidden to drink alcohol, by both religion and the state, although the law permits non-Muslims to drink.

▶ *A Chinese family enjoying a traditional bowl of tea in Kuala Lumpur.*

## Religion

As a multicultural society Malaysia enjoys a blend of religions, and people are free to follow whatever beliefs they choose. Just over half the population are Muslim and mosques are a common sight all over the country. Chinese Malaysians tend to be Buddhist or Taoist, while most of the Indian population is Hindu. Around 8 per cent of people are Christian and some minority groups still follow their traditional animist religions, with rituals that are led by village elders or shamans.

▶ *At the Hindu festival of Thaipusam in Kuala Lipis, people smash coconuts in front of a procession to honour Lord Subriaman.*

## IN THEIR OWN WORDS

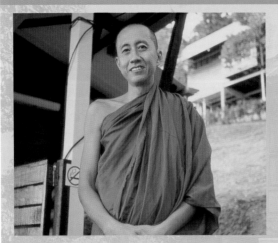

'My name is Bhante Aggacitta and I am from Taiping. I've been a Buddhist monk since 1978. I was not satisfied with what the world was offering me. I left Malaysia for 13 years, and then spent a further seven years on a remote mountain with no contact with anybody. When I finally came down I was shocked by what I saw! One person had this small round machine that took shiny discs. I had no idea what it was, and was amazed when I found that it could play music. They called it a CD player!'

## Call to prayer

Islamic law is not followed by Malaysian society as fervently as it is in some Arab and African Muslim countries. Women have a lot of freedom in Malaysia, unlike women in many other Muslim countries. Malays still keep to customs that were in use before Islam was brought to the region, such as consulting the *bomoh*. In some areas the traditional Malay wedding still follows the old Hindu ceremony and there is generally great tolerance of other religions. Young people across the country appear less interested in religion than the older generations.

Ramadan is one Muslim tradition that affects the entire country. This is a holy month, and everyone in Malaysia is mindful and respectful of the Ramadan time of year. During Ramadan all Muslims fast from sun-up to sundown for a whole month. They break their fast with food and drink at sunset.

▼ *Muslim men at prayer in a mosque on Pinang island.*

# 8

# Changes at Work

### Rapid progress

Employment opportunities have become much wider for Malaysians as the country's economy has developed. Traditionally people used to have a choice between subsistence farming or working in plantations and mines. People would start work very early in the morning and finish at midday to escape the heat of the afternoon.

◀ These days there are thousands of office workers in Malaysia's cities. Modern international-style cafés are popular lunchtime venues for businesspeople.

Industrial, urban and social development has dramatically altered the options for young Malaysians. There are jobs in businesses producing raw materials such as natural gas and palm oil, and in manufacturing industries. A wide array of jobs in service industries such as transport, tourism and entertainment are available. Most people now go to work at 8 a.m. and leave at 4 p.m. Today only 18 per cent of people are employed in agriculture, forestry and fishing. A third work in industry and half in services. Unemployment is low, with only 3 per cent of the workforce unable to find work in 2003.

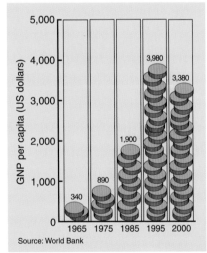

Source: World Bank

▲ Malaysia's GNP has risen dramatically over the last 20 years, although the 1997 recession meant that growth slowed down.

# IN THEIR OWN WORDS

'My name is Shaz. I studied catering at college before starting work at this restaurant in Kuala Lumpur. The tourist industry and restaurant business have been suffering recently. The world seems to be going through some changes at the moment, and fewer people are travelling because of worries about terrorism. Fortunately, Malaysia attracts tourists even just on a stopover to other places and it seems safe here. We have a mixture of tourists and locals in here, which is good because it means we don't have to rely on just one type of customer. Local people like to come here to show off a bit. I suppose you could call us a lifestyle restaurant!'

## Tiger economy

Malaysia is one of the countries that economists call the 'tiger' economies. These are the Asian countries that showed amazing rates of development and financial growth during the 1980s and 1990s. All the tiger economies suffered from a recession called the Asian economic crisis, which began in 1997. Although growth slowed down, Malaysia adapted more quickly than other countries, and its main industries are productive once again. Most of the people who lost their jobs in 1997–98 are back at work, and people continue to leave behind their small plots of farmland to find jobs in the cities. The economy is growing again and around 10 per cent of workers are now employed in the construction of new buildings or facilities.

▼ *An old cycle trishaw beside its modern replacement, the taxi.*

### Industrial drive

Since the 1970s Malaysia has made much progress in developing its industries. The Malaysian prime minister Mahathir Mohamad led the way, taking personal charge of one of the country's successes, the Proton car. When he announced in 1983 that Malaysia would start making cars, many people did not believe it would be possible. Now, however, the Proton company exports to 50 countries and has bought the British carmaker Lotus.

▲ *The manager of a salesroom for Proton, the national carmaker.*

Since the early 1980s Malaysia has become one of the world's largest producers of disk drives and other electronic components. The country's leaders now want companies to invent and improve, rather than simply assembling electronics. The government is investing billions of dollars to create a light industrial and business zone – the Multimedia Super Corridor – where companies can help Malaysia to become a world leader in high-tech industry.

◀ *Cyberjaya, in the Multimedia Super Corridor, has been planned as the business centre for the IT industry but its growth has been slowed by the poor economic situation that affected Asia in the late 1990s.*

# IN THEIR OWN WORDS

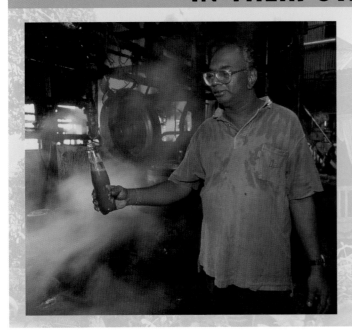

'I'm Mr Mahadhevan, the supervisor in this palm oil mill in Taiping. Although there has been little change here, other oil mills are much more modern. The palm fruit comes here in big trucks from plantations nearby. We have to cook the fruit and then squeeze the oil out of it – it's a simple process really. The oil is then loaded into tankers and taken away to another factory to be refined. It's a real growth industry with many new palm plantations taking over from rubber trees. This kind of oil is used for many things. A lot of it goes to make margarine, but now they are experimenting on using it for cars.'

## Thriving mineral industries

In its drive to develop new markets, Malaysia has not abandoned the traditional industries. Tin mines and other mineral concessions are still working. Tin production fell from 70,000 metric tonnes of concentrates in the early 1970s to about 6,307 tonnes in 2000. This fall was mainly because the price paid for tin around the world was very low, but more tin will be mined when prices climb again.

Malaysians are proud of the country's achievements and the government encourages people to support national industries and work for unity.

▶ *The Petronas company is very important to Malaysia's economy. It is famous worldwide and even runs a Formula 1 racing team.*

### Destination Malaysia

The tourism sector has enormous potential for Malaysia, which is South-east Asia's biggest destination. The country started to get many more visitors after its Visit Malaysia Year campaign in 1990. Most popular with tourists are Kuala Lumpur and the country's beautiful islands. Langkawi and Tioman islands are famous for their beaches, while Sipadan, a small island off Borneo, is one of the world's most important diving sites. Malacca and Pinang attract people interested in historical sites, while ecotourism is a new and expanding industry; people visit the national parks for wildlife treks and caving adventures.

The tourism industry currently has some problems though. Pollution and development are spoiling some holiday destinations, while fear of terrorism has stopped many people from travelling altogether.

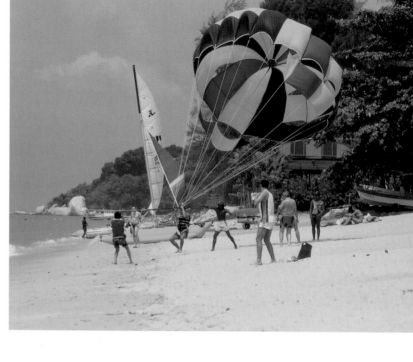

▲ *The resort of Batu Ferringhi, on Pinang Island, attracts many tourists as it has excellent watersports facilities.*

## IN THEIR OWN WORDS

'I'm Appu, a tour guide in Kuala Lipis. Sometimes we get lots of tourists and then other years just a few – international events seem to affect how many people travel. I often feel like I'm in a one-man fight to develop the ecotourism market. Tourists love the national parks where they can see protected wild animals and amazing plants, but we haven't developed a good system yet. We preserve areas of forest, but nobody has thought about how to market them to tourists. By attracting tourists we can prove that we can earn money from the forests without chopping them down – and this way is sustainable.'

## Getting about

Malaysia's national airline has a good reputation and its service has been boosted by the new Kuala Lumpur international airport at Sepang, at the southern end of the Multimedia Super Corridor. The airport has become a regional hub, with people who are travelling long distances using Malaysia as a place where they can change planes and even stop over for a quick visit.

The country's good road network means that many visitors come from neighbouring countries, especially Singapore and Thailand. The railway system, established by the British, has evolved into one of the finest in Asia and it employs many people. The line carries passengers from Singapore to Bangkok, with the Malaysian section being the most comfortable.

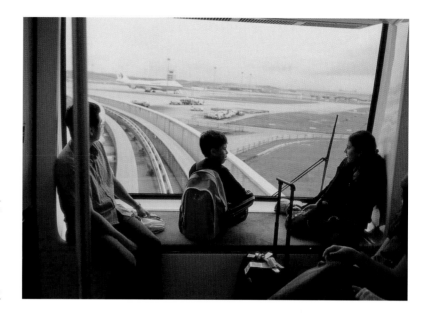

▲ Kuala Lumpur's new airport has an automatic shuttle train.

▼ New infrastructure projects, like this one in Putrajaya, help to improve the transport of goods.

## Shopping heaven

Big shopping centres have sprouted up alongside old-style bazaars, or indoor markets, in Malaysia's towns and cities. International chain stores and restaurants are now common in big malls such as the spectacular Mines Shopping Fair, 15 km from Kuala Lumpur. A day trip to a mall is a popular pastime for young people and families, and the malls provide many jobs.

In rural areas, people still lead a more traditional life and everyone must share the chores in the house and fields. Most food and household products are bought and sold in markets across the country. Night bazaars or *pasar malams* are popular with both local people buying groceries and tourists looking for gifts, handicrafts or special goods. It is ethnic Chinese people who do most of this kind of business in Malaysia.

▲ Although Malaysia is a mainly Muslim nation, Christmas shopping is still big business.

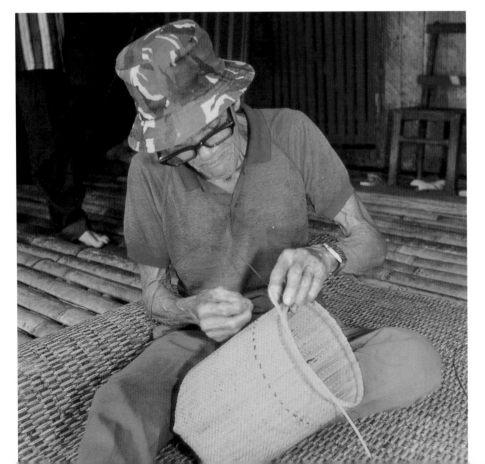

◄ An old man in a rural village making a traditional bamboo basket.

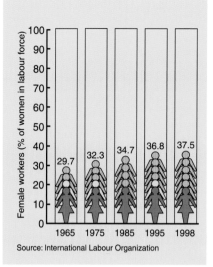

## Women at work

Convenience stores and supermarkets have also become a common sight in the cities, and many women work in this sector. Women have always done much of the retail work in South-east Asia, but the modernization of shopping in Malaysia has meant that such women are learning new skills, such as marketing and shop design. Every year more women go to work, many of them in retail shops or restaurants. The number of female shop managers is also on the increase.

▲ *Nearly 40 per cent of Malaysia's working population are women.*

Source: International Labour Organization

◄ *Both Malaysian business women and female students are experiencing social and economic changes that are widening the areas in which they are able to work.*

# IN THEIR OWN WORDS

'My name is Harry Bong, and I'm a culture and art specialist from Kuala Lumpur. We seem to have forgotten our own culture and heritage in the rush to be modern and rich. Of course, as the nation develops, things must change, but the recent changes have been so rapid that some people seem to have forgotten to value their own history. It's really about being Malaysian! The past should always give us a reference for the future and that is why I promote traditional art and modern art in my gallery. Many kids have never been to an art gallery and don't know what our ancestors created.'

# 9

# The Way Ahead

The Asian economic crisis of 1997–98 provided a strong test of the progress Malaysia has made since independence. Many people thought that the government would struggle to keep the country peaceful and stable as the economy declined. Political problems did occur and the deputy prime minister, Anwar Ibrahim, was sent to prison accused of corruption and social crimes. However, the economy bounced back after a period of strict controls.

## Looking to the future

Malaysia does have problems to overcome, notably in the areas of energy production and the environment, but the huge investments that the country has made in education and technology should stand it in good stead for the future. Malaysia is a growing economic and cultural presence in the world. It held the Commonwealth Games in 1998, and a new racetrack at Sepang hosts Formula 1 and motorcycle

▲ *The giant telecom tower rising above Kuala Lumpur is a testament to Malaysia's modern technological advance.*

◄ *The city of Putrajaya is being built close to Kuala Lumpur. It will eventually become the new capital.*

grands prix. The country takes a strong role regionally as a founding member of ASEAN, the Association of South East Asian Nations, and it now gives technological aid to some of its neighbours. Malaysia seems to be on course to keep developing into a prosperous multicultural nation that other Asian countries can look to as an example.

▶ *The education system in Malaysia will provide these students with good opportunities for the future.*

# IN THEIR OWN WORDS

'I'm Azlan Hajijohan and I'm 18 years old. I am running this Internet and computer repair shop for my brother, who has gone to work in Kuala Lumpur. He taught me about computers, and I learned a lot myself as well – it's not difficult. I want to go and study IT engineering at a special multimedia university in Cyberjaya, which is just for studying computers. If you don't know about computers you really can't do anything now. People in Malaysia have opened their eyes and we can be a centre for computer excellence.'

# Glossary

**Aboriginal** This means coming from the original or first people to inhabit a country. It is most commonly used to refer to the original peoples of Australia, but can be used to mean the first people in any area.

**Animist** Animist religions are traditional systems of belief based on the idea of spirits that inhabit and protect natural areas, objects and people.

**ASEAN** The Association of South East Asian Nations. A trade association that includes ten countries in South-east Asia: Malaysia, Thailand, Indonesia, Singapore, Philippines, Brunei, Vietnam, Myanmar, Lao PDR and Cambodia.

**Bahasa Malayu** The main language of Malaysia, which is similar to the Bahasa Indonesia spoken in neighbouring Indonesia.

**Biomass fuel** A fuel made from crops and plants.

**Bomoh** The Malay word for a shaman (see below).

**Cash crops** Crops that are grown to be sold, often to other countries, instead of being grown for the farmer to eat.

**Cassava** A tropical plant. Its roots, which contain a lot of starch, can be eaten and used to make tapioca.

**Commonwealth Games** A major sports event similar to the Olympics but involving only countries that are members of the British Commonwealth.

**Conurbation** When two or more towns grow so big that they meet each other, the urban area that they make up is called a conurbation.

**Deforestation** The clearing of forests, which are then replaced by other land types.

**Ecotourism** A growing sector of the tourism industry aimed at people who travel to see nature and are often more interested in conservation than beaches or nightlife.

**Federal union** A system of government in which several states unite into one country or federation while the states still control some laws and policy independently.

**Fossil fuels** Fuels such as coal and oil, made from the remains of ancient forests, found deep underground or under the sea.

**GNP** Gross National Product, the amount of money Malaysia makes from all the goods and services it provides.

**Hardwoods** Heavy and expensive types of wood, such as mahogany and teak, that last for a long time.

**Herblore** Traditional knowledge of plants and their medicinal uses.

**Hub** Just as the hub of a wheel is its central point, a 'transport hub' is a place where people from many destinations can find connections to other places they need to get to.

**Hydroelectric power** Electricity generated by turbines that are turned by the force of falling water.

**Infrastructure** The network of transport links, communication links and power supplies that a country needs to have in order for its economy to work well.

**Kernel** The soft centre of a nut or a fruit stone.

**Logging** Cutting down the trees in a forest in order to use, or sell, the wood.

**Longhouse** Certain ethnic groups in East Malaysia still live in their traditional longhouses, which are raised on stilts and sometimes home to the entire village.

**Malay** The biggest ethnic group in Malaysia. Malays are nearly all Muslim.

**Malaya** The pre-independence name for Malaysia.

**Mangrove** A tropical tree that grows in swamps and sends roots down from its branches.

**Monsoon** A seasonal wind that blows in from the oceans, bringing with it heavy rain.

**Peninsula** An area of land almost surrounded by water, but connected to another larger piece of land.

**Peninsular Malaysia** Also called West Malaysia, the part of Malaysia connected to the Asian mainland – the more populated and developed part of the country.

**Recession** A period when the economy declines, meaning that companies find it difficult to sell their goods for a profit and many people are out of work.

**Resin** A thick white liquid that oozes out of rubber trees.

**Semiconductor plants** Factories making devices used in electronic equipment.

**Shaman** A person in the community who studies the animist spirits and communicates with them at special rituals or ceremonies.

**Slash-and-burn** A method of farming in which an area of trees and bushes is cut down and the vegetation is burned. The ash that is produced makes the land fertile for crops.

**Smog** A mixture of smoke and fog, or, air pollution caused when sunlight reacts with chemicals in vehicle exhausts.

**Subsistence farming** Subsistence farmers grow only enough crops and raise animals in order to feed themselves and their families, rather than growing large amounts to sell.

**Sustainable** Able to last for a long time.

**World oil crisis, 1973** In 1973 the main crude-oil-producing countries in the Middle East made an agreement to stop selling oil until the countries that imported oil agreed to pay a higher price for it.

# Further Information

## Books for younger readers

*Malaysia* by Heidi Munan (Marshall Cavendish, 1990)

*Malaysia* by Jonathan Rowell (Raintree Steck-Vaughn, 1997)

*Malaysia (Economically Developing Countries)* by Jonathan Rowell (Hodder Wayland, 2001)

*Wealth of Nations: Malaysia* by Jen Green (Hodder Wayland, 2001)

## Books for older readers and teachers

*A History of Malaysia, 2nd edn* by Barbara Watson Andaya and Leonard Y. Andaya (University of Hawaii Press, 2001)

*Cultural Sites of Malaysia, Singapore, and Indonesia* by Jacques Dumarçay and Michael Smithies (Oxford University Press, 1998)

*They Came to Malaya: A Travellers' Anthology* by J. M. Gullick (Oxford University Press, 1995)

*Historical Dictionary of Malaysia, 2nd edn.* by Amarjit Kaur (Scarecrow, 2001)

*The Shaping of Malaysia, (eds)* by Amarjit Kaur and Ian Metcalfe (St Martin's Press, 1998)

## Useful Addresses

High Commission of Malaysia
45–46 Belgrave Square
London SW1X 8QT
Tel: 020 7235 8033

## Places to visit

Commonwealth Institute
Kensington High Street
London W8 6NQ
Tel: 020 7603 4535

The British Empire & Commonwealth Museum
Station Approach
Temple Meads
Bristol BS1 6QH
Tel: 0117 925 4980 Fax: 0117 925 4983
E-mail: admin@empiremuseum.co.uk

# Index

Page numbers in **bold** refer to photographs, maps or statistics panels.